KB276133

Stories of
Sherlock Holmes

Happy House

About Wise & Wide

- A systematic 6-level English reading program based on Lexile® measures
- Diverse and interesting topics chosen from the elementary curriculums of Korea and English speaking western countries
- Well-written books in various forms including fiction stories, descriptive texts, and classics retold
- The informative but original fiction stories grab your interest, leading to the easy and clear understanding of the educational content.
- Improve thinking skills with solid after-reading activities at all levels of the series.

Wise & Wide is a 6-level English reading program that consists of 60 books and each level is systematically divided by Lexile® measures. The Lexile® Framework for Reading is the most popular reading measuring system in American formal education curriculums and many English programs. Over 20 out of 50 states in the U.S. mark Lexile® measures directly on students' final report cards and over 300 well-known publishers adopt and use Lexile® measures.

Experience many kinds of readings written by professional writers from the U.S. and England. They used interesting topics that were carefully chosen after analyzing elementary curriculums from around the world including Korea, the U.S., England, and Australia among many others. Comprehensive after-reading activities including graphic organizers, speaking tasks, and After-reading Tests are ready for you.

Levels in the series and their corresponding Lexile® measures

Level	Lexile® measures	U.S. Grade
Level 1	Below 200L	Pre K - K
Level 2	190L - 400L	Lower Grade 1
Level 3	350L - 530L	Upper Grade 1
Level 4	420L - 650L	Grade 2
Level 5	520L - 940L	Grade 3 - 4
Level 6	830L - 1070L	Grade 5 - 6

* Smart Readers: Wise & Wide level 1 is applicable to the preschool level in the U.S.

* The source of the relationship between Lexile® measures and U.S. school grades: CCSS(Common Core State Standards) FOR ENGLISH LANGUAGE ARTS, APPENDIX A (2012, which is used by 45 states in the U.S.)

Topic List

	Level 1	Level 2	Level 3	Level 4	Level 5	Level 6
Book 1	Science>Biology: The hibernation of animals Story	Science>Biology: Living and nonliving things Story	Science>Biology> Animals & the Environment: Sea otters Story	Environment> Living with nature: The diver & the persimmon tree Story	Science>Biology> Animal: Amazing animals of the Amazon Story	Science>Biology: Germs, transmitted diseases Story
Book 2	Literature> World classics: Aesop's fables Story	Literature> Traditional fairy tale: Old tales about stones Story	Social Studies> Economy: To run a business to make and save money Story	Science>Biology> Plants: Photosynthesis Story	Science>Earth science: Earth's layers, earthquakes, volcanoes, and earth's atmosphere Report	Mathematics> Sequence: The golden ratio & the Fibonacci sequence Story
Book 3	Science>Physics: How shadows are formed Story	Literature> World classics: Peter Pan Story	Science>Scientific technology: Nanobots Story	Literature>Myths: World's creation stories Story	Literature> Legend: The story of King Arthur Story	Literature>Myths: Constellation myths Story
Book 4	Literature> Traditional literature: The Talmud Story	Science>Biology> Animal: Polar bears Story	Science>Biology> Animal: Mountain gorillas Story	Social Studies> Cultural anthropology: Amazing ancient cultures of the world Story	Science> Earth science: Clouds and weather Story	Literature> Human & animals: The friendship between a girl and a horse Story
Book 5	Social Studies> Ethics: Rules in daily life Story	Science>Biology: The five senses Report	Social Studies> Cultural anthropology: Astonishing festivals Report	Art>Music: Stories from two operas Story	Social Studies> World culture & history: The Renaissance Story	Sports> Board sports: Surfing & snowboarding Story
Book 6	Social Studies> World geography & travel: Tourist attractions around the world Story	Science>Biology> Animal: Dinosaurs Story	Science> Astronomy: The solar system Story	Social Studies> People: Three great people who overcame hardships Story	Science>Scientific technology: The wonderful world of robots Report	Art>Music: Composers of the Romantic Era Report
Book 7	Science> Space science: The life of astronauts Report	Social Studies> Cultural anthropology: Mythological monsters from around the world Report	Mathematics> Elementary mathematics: Numbers, measurement, shapes and data Report	Science & Social Studies> Technology & culture: Inventions from around the world Report	Art>Works of art: Famous paintings Report	Social Studies> Human & animals: Animals in action for human Report
Book 8	Social Studies> Cultural anthropology: Various living cultures of the world Story	Art>Music: Instruments in the orchestra Story	Social Studies> Life safety: Learning and using outdoor survival skills Story	Social Studies> History: The California Gold Rush Report	Social Studies & Science> Psychology: Psychology in everyday life Story	Literature> World classics: The Merchant of Venice Story
Book 9	Social Studies> Jobs: Interviews about jobs Report	Science>Scientific technology: Developments in technology in different times Story	Social Studies> Politics>Election: Running for 3rd grade class president Story	Literature> World classics: Stories of Sherlock Holmes Story	Literature> World classics: Adrift in the Pacific Story	Social Studies> History & People: Great world leaders in history Report
Book 10	Literature>Traditional fairy tale: Eastern and Western folk tales on the same theme Story	Sports>Winter sports: Various aspects of some Winter Olympic sports Report	Literature> World classics: Short stories by O. Henry Story	Sports> Ball games: Various aspects of popular ball games Report	Social Studies> History: Famous events that changed world history Report	Art & Social Studies> Art: Stories about the creation, distribution, and preservation of paintings Report

* 10 books in each level will be published.

How to Use This Book

• Before Reading

You can easily find the topic and what kind of story you are about to read.

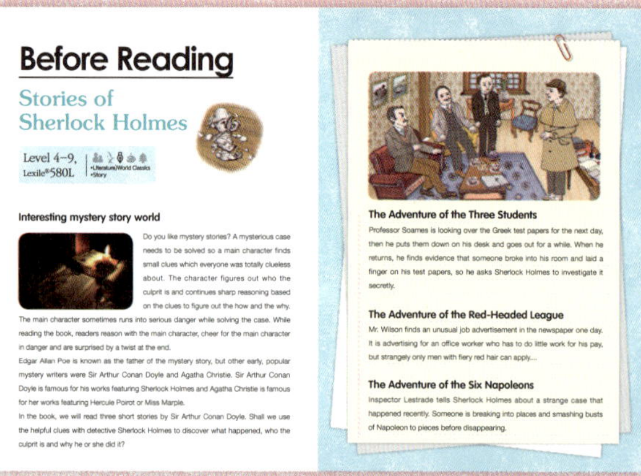

• The text

All the stories were written by professional writers from the U.S. and England, so you will read authentic and appropriate English sentences and expressions in every book in the series.

• Pop Quiz

Check out right away if you understand what you have just read by solving a pop quiz that checks your comprehension.

• Key Words

The key words and expressions on each page are listed for you to easily study them.

• Aha! Tips

Download free Korean explanations at *www.ihappyhouse.co.kr* for all of the sentences marked with "Aha!". These explain cultural, scientific, and economic knowledge or they deal with aspects of English such as grammatical structures or idiomatic expressions. There are lots of "Aha! Tips" to help you understand the text.

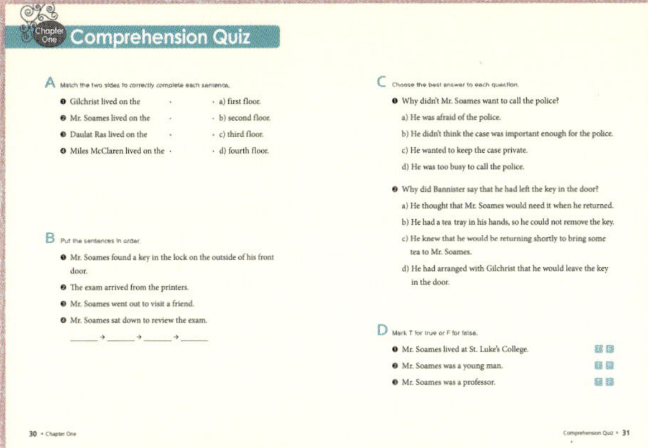

•Comprehension Quiz

After reading one chapter, solve various questions to find out if you fully understand the content.

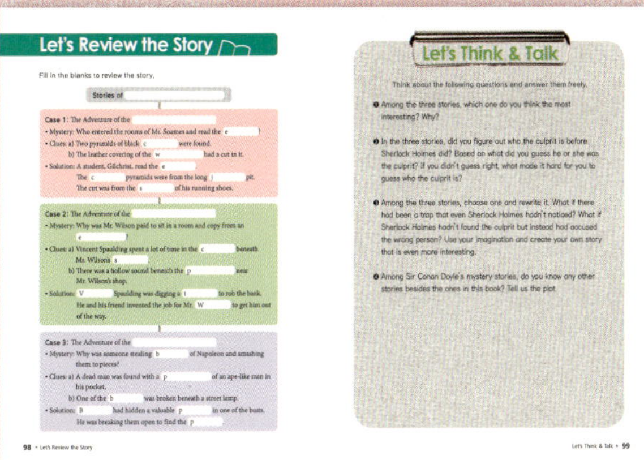

•Let's Review the Story / •Let's Think & Talk

Fill in the blanks in the organizer to summarize the whole story. Express your own thinking and feelings about the story by answering the questions. You can build up logic and reasoning skills for your essay examinations in the future.

Appendix

Audio CD

In the CD audio book form, the texts are read vividly by American professional voice actors.
(MP3 files downloaded for free)

After-reading Test

Solve an additionally provided After-reading Test for each book.

The Korean translation, Answer Keys, a Word Quiz, a Word List, and Aha! Tips for each book

You can download them for free at *www.ihappyhouse.co.kr* or *www.darakwon.co.kr*

Before Reading

Stories of Sherlock Holmes

Level 4–9,
Lexile®580L

•Literature〉World Classics
•Story

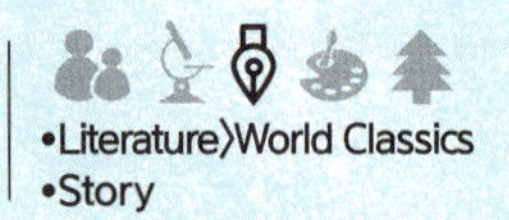

Interesting mystery story world

Do you like mystery stories? A mysterious case needs to be solved so a main character finds small clues which everyone was totally clueless about. The character figures out who the culprit is and continues sharp reasoning based on the clues to figure out the how and the why.

The main character sometimes runs into serious danger while solving the case. While reading the book, readers reason with the main character, cheer for the main character in danger and are surprised by a twist at the end.

Edgar Allan Poe is known as the father of the mystery story, but other early, popular mystery writers were Sir Arthur Conan Doyle and Agatha Christie. Sir Arthur Conan Doyle is famous for his works featuring Sherlock Holmes and Agatha Christie is famous for her works featuring Hercule Poirot or Miss Marple.

In the book, we will read three short stories by Sir Arthur Conan Doyle. Shall we use the helpful clues with detective Sherlock Holmes to discover what happened, who the culprit is and why he or she did it?

The Adventure of the Three Students

Professor Soames is looking over the Greek test papers for the next day, then he puts them down on his desk and goes out for a while. When he returns, he finds evidence that someone broke into his room and laid a finger on his test papers, so he asks Sherlock Holmes to investigate it secretly.

The Adventure of the Red-Headed League

Mr. Wilson finds an unusual job advertisement in the newspaper one day. It is advertising for an office worker who has to do little work for his pay, but strangely only men with fiery red hair can apply....

The Adventure of the Six Napoleons

Inspector Lestrade tells Sherlock Holmes about a strange case that happened recently. Someone is breaking into places and smashing busts of Napoleon to pieces before disappearing.

Contents

Stories of Sherlock Holmes

Stories of
Sherlock Holmes

221B
The Creator of
Sherlock Holmes

Sir Arthur Conan Doyle was a Scottish writer, who was born in 1859.

He was also a doctor, and spent some time working as a surgeon on board a ship.

In addition, he studied botany at the Royal Botanic Garden in Edinburgh.

▲ Sir Arthur Conan Doyle

Despite being so busy, he wrote short stories in his spare time.

During his life, he wrote many kinds of stories, including fantasy and science fiction.

He also wrote nonfiction and poetry.

KEY WORDS

- creator
- Sir
- Scottish
- **be born** (*cf*. bear(bear-bore-born))
- **spend** (spend-spent-spent)
- **work as** (*cf*. work)
- surgeon
- on board a ship
- in addition
- botany
- Royal Botanic Garden
- Edinburgh
- despite
- spare
- during one's life
- kind
- fantasy
- science fiction
- nonfiction
- poetry

But Conan Doyle's best-known stories have always been about crime and mysteries.

His first published story was called *The Mystery of Sasassa Valley*.

It was set in Africa, perhaps inspired by his travels.

He wrote a series of novels about a scientist called Professor Challenger.

One of these novels, *The Lost World* was made into a movie several times between 1925 and 2001.

▲ a statue of Sherlock Holmes situated outside Baker Street underground station in London

▲ Sir Arthur Conan Doyle's grave at Minstead, England. "Steel True, Blade Straight" is inscribed on his gravestone.

KEY WORDS

- best-known
- crime
- mystery
- publish
- be set in (set-set-set)
- perhaps
- inspire
- travel
- a series of
- novel
- professor
- challenger
- be made into (make-made-made)
- several

The most famous character invented by Doyle is Sherlock Holmes.

Sherlock Holmes is a fictional detective who lives at 221B Baker Street in London.

He solves difficult mysteries with the help of his friend, Dr. Watson.

Holmes and Watson appear in four novels and fifty-six short stories.

Many of these have also been made into movies or TV series.

Most of these stories take place in the late nineteenth century or early twentieth century. Here are three of those stories.

Dr. Watson is the narrator.

The Adventure of the Three Students

An Intruder at the College

This case took place in 1895.

Sherlock Holmes and I were staying in an English university town.

One evening, a middle-aged man called Mr. Soames came to call on us.

He was a professor at the nearby St. Luke's College.

He seemed to be very upset.

It was clear that something unusual had happened.

"Mr. Holmes, I hope that you can help me," he said.

"I am very busy just now," said Holmes.

"Why don't you call the police instead?"

"Oh no, I can't do that," said Mr. Soames.

"I want to keep this matter private.

I hope you can solve it as it could be rather embarrassing for myself and the college."

Sherlock Holmes listened while Mr. Soames told his story.

"Tomorrow is exam day at the college," he began.

"The exams are kept secret.

Students must not see them before tomorrow.

Today, around 3 p.m., the Greek exam arrived from the printer. It consisted of three separate pages.

I began to review the exam in my study, but did not finish the task.

I had promised to visit a friend at 4:30 p.m. I left the pages on my desk and went out for about an hour.

When I returned, I found a key in my front door, sticking out of the lock on the outside.

My servant, Bannister, said that he had left it there by mistake.

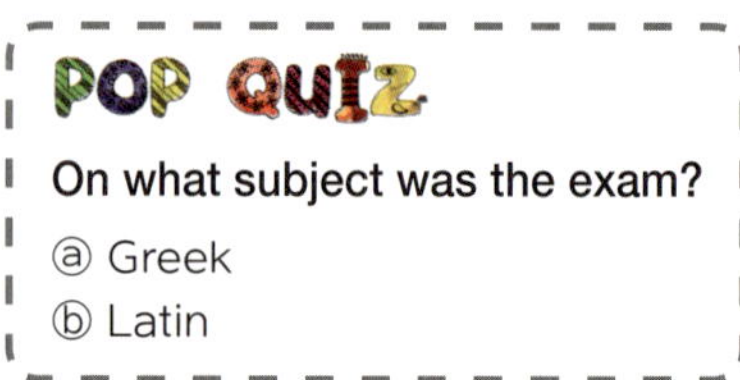

KEY WORDS

- secret
- around
- Greek
- printer
- consist of
- separate
- review

- study
- task
- leave (leave-left-left)
- front door
- stick out of (stick-stuck-stuck)
- servant
- by mistake

- as soon as
- lie (lie-lay-lain)
- side table
- still
- carefully
- sit forward (sit-sat-sat)
- continue

As soon as I looked at my desk, I knew that someone
had looked at the exam.

I had left all three pages together.

Now, one of them was lying on the floor.

Another was on a side table near the window.

The third was still on the desk."

Holmes had been listening carefully.

Now, he sat forward in his chair as Mr. Soames
continued with his story.

"I wondered if Bannister had been looking at the pages, but he denied it.

In fact, he was so upset that he nearly fainted.

He stood in the doorway and then collapsed into a chair by the window while I searched the room.

I soon discovered some other strange things.

I have a new writing table, which is covered in smooth, red leather.

There was a cut in it about three inches long.

I also found a small pyramid of black clay.

It had specks of sawdust in it.

Mr. Holmes, I do hope you can help me. 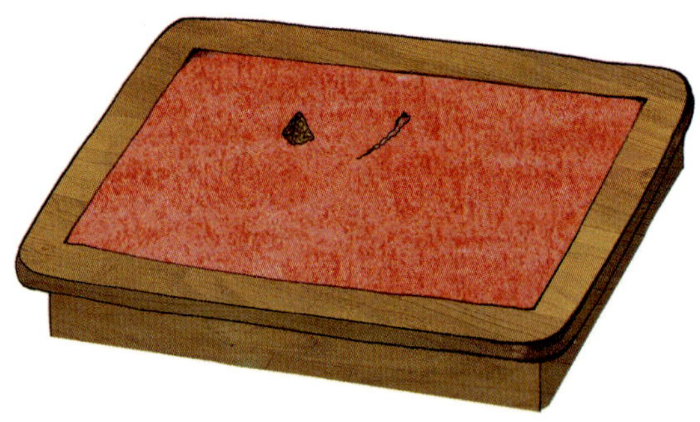

If not, I shall have to cancel the exam until a new one can be written."

Holmes stood up and put on his coat.

"Let us visit your rooms to see what we can discover!

Watson, you may come too if you wish."

Mr. Soames lived in the college.

His rooms consisted of the study and a small bedroom next door.

His rooms were on the first floor.

Above were three more floors.

A different student lived on each floor.

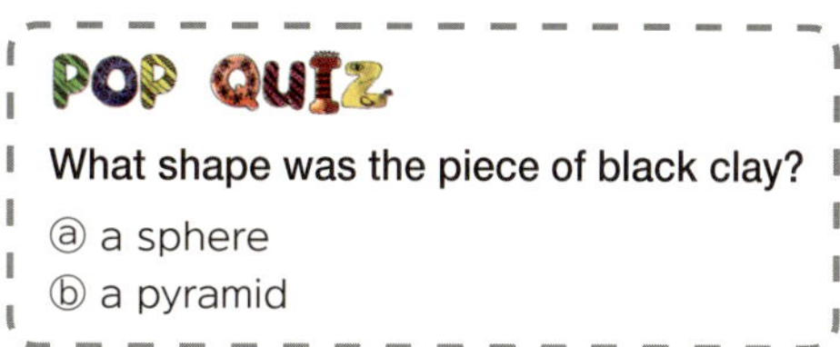

KEY WORDS

- wonder if
- deny
- in fact
- so ... that ~
- nearly
- faint
- doorway
- collapse

- search
- discover
- be covered in
- leather
- cut
- inch (1inch = 2.54cm)
- pyramid
- clay

- speck
- sawdust
- if not
- have to + *Verb*
- cancel
- put on (put-put-put)
- floor
- above

We approached from the courtyard outside.

Holmes stopped at Mr. Soames' window.

He stood on tiptoe and looked inside the room.

Mr. Soames laughed.

"I don't think anyone could have gotten in through that
window," he said.

"It's too small."

He led us through an archway to the bottom of a
staircase.

His door opened off the staircase, which led up to the
rooms of the three students.

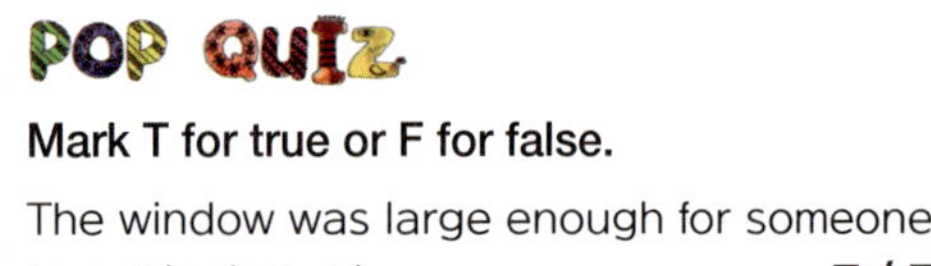

Mark T for true or F for false.

The window was large enough for someone
to get in through.   T / F

KEY WORDS

- approach
- courtyard
- stand on tiptoe (stand-stood-stood)
  (*cf.* tiptoe)
- get in (get-got-gotten/got)
- lead (lead-led-led)(*cf.* lead up to)
- archway
- bottom
- staircase

- open off
- unlock (↔ lock)
- let ~ in
- must have + *p.p.*
- recover
- since
- no longer
- point to
- next to

He unlocked the door and let us in.

"Where is Bannister?" asked Holmes.

"He must have recovered, since he is no longer here. Which chair was he sitting in when you left him?"

"This one."

Mr. Soames pointed to a chair near the window, next to the side table.

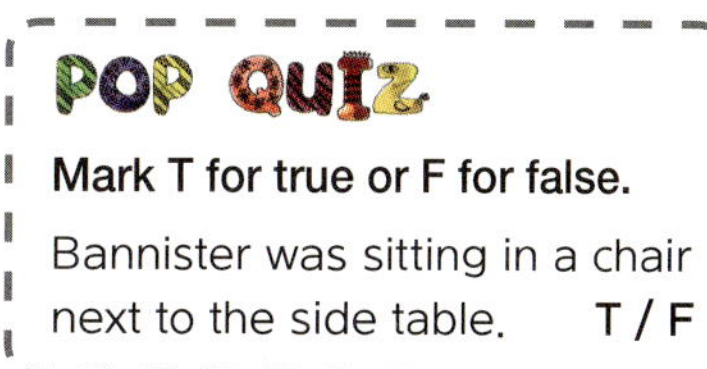

"I think the intruder brought the pages to this table to copy them," said Holmes.

"He wanted a good view out of the window to see you coming back."

"But I came back into the building through a side entrance," said Mr. Soames.

"You must have disturbed him when you came back," said Holmes.

"He left in a hurry and did not have time to put the
pages back on the desk."

Holmes moved to the writing table to examine the cut.

He also picked up the small pyramid of black clay.

"What is through that door?" he asked, pointing.

"My bedroom," said Mr. Soames.

With permission from Mr. Soames, Holmes went into
the bedroom.

There, he found another small pyramid of black clay,
just like the first.

The intruder had been in the bedroom as well.

POP QUIZ

What did Holmes find in Mr. Soames' bedroom?
ⓐ a small pyramid of black clay
ⓑ a small pyramid of sawdust

KEY WORDS

- copy
- view
- entrance
- disturb

- in a hurry
- put ~ back
- examine
- pick up

- permission
- just like
- as well

"Tell me about the students who live in the rooms above yours," said Holmes.

"On the floor above me lives a young man named Gilchrist," said Mr. Soames.

"He is a fine athlete, who is very good at the long jump."

Mr. Soames went on to tell us about the student on the third floor.

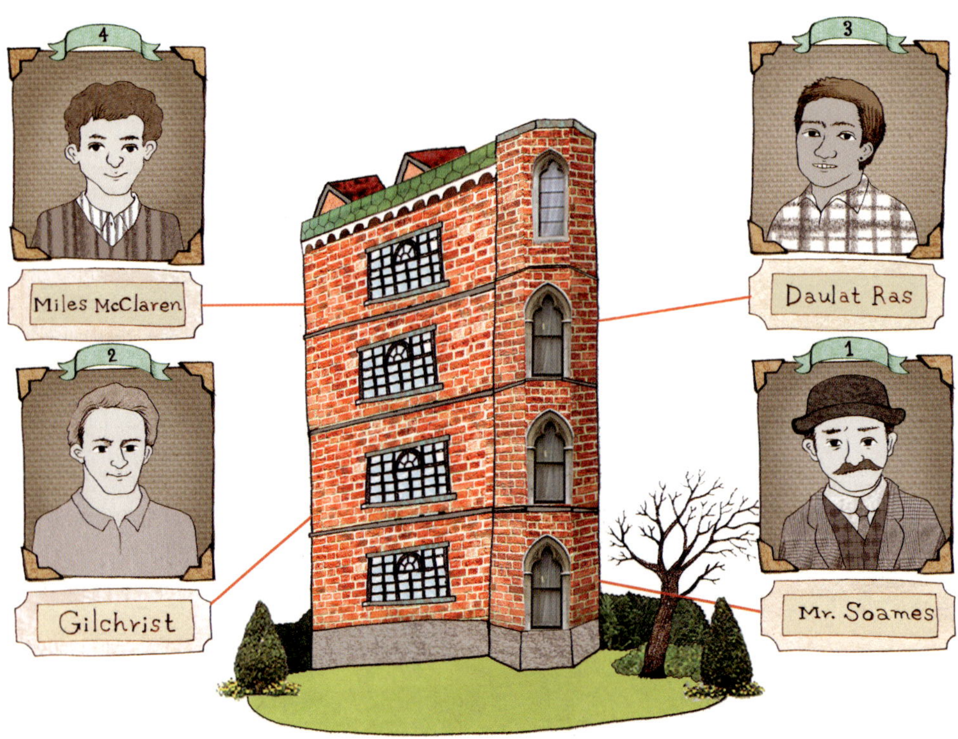

"An Indian man lives there. His name is Daulat Ras.

He is a quiet man and works hard, though Greek is his

weak subject.

The top floor belongs to Miles McClaren. 

He is extremely clever but very lazy.

He has done very little this term.

He must be worried about this exam."

"Do you suspect him?" asked Holmes.

Mr. Soames nodded. "Of the three, he is the most likely

one."

POP QUIZ

Mr. Soames suspected __________ .

ⓐ Miles McClaren

ⓑ Daulat Ras

KEY WORDS

- name
- fine
- athlete
- be good at
- long jump
- go on to + *Verb* (go-went-gone)
- Indian
- quiet
- though
- subject
- belong to + *Noun(Person, Object)*
- extremely
- term
- worried
- suspect
- nod
- likely

Holmes asked Mr. Soames to fetch his servant, Bannister.
The man was short with a white face, and was around
fifty years old.

"Why did you leave the key in the front door?" asked
Holmes.

"I came here to bring Mr. Soames some tea," said
Bannister.

"When I saw that he wasn't here, I left at once.
I left the key in the door because I had a tea tray in my
hands.
I intended to come back for it, but I forgot."

Holmes pointed at the chair near the window.

"When you felt faint, why did you sit over there?" he asked.

"There were other chairs much closer to you."

"I don't know. It didn't matter which chair it was," said Bannister.

"I just wanted to sit down."

Mr. Soames gave us some further information about the students.

We learned that Gilchrist was the tallest of the three.

At this, Holmes declared that he would return home.

I went with him and we had a fine supper.

But I was still no closer to solving the mystery.

Comprehension Quiz

A Match the two sides to correctly complete each sentence.

❶ Gilchrist lived on the •   • a) first floor.

❷ Mr. Soames lived on the •   • b) second floor.

❸ Daulat Ras lived on the •   • c) third floor.

❹ Miles McClaren lived on the •   • d) fourth floor.

B Put the sentences in order.

❶ Mr. Soames found a key in the lock on the outside of his front door.

❷ The exam arrived from the printers.

❸ Mr. Soames went out to visit a friend.

❹ Mr. Soames sat down to review the exam.

_______ → _______ → _______ → _______

 Choose the best answer to each question.

❶ Why didn't Mr. Soames want to call the police?

a) He was afraid of the police.

b) He didn't think the case was important enough for the police.

c) He wanted to keep the case private.

d) He was too busy to call the police.

❷ Why did Bannister say that he had left the key in the door?

a) He thought that Mr. Soames would need it when he returned.

b) He had a tea tray in his hands, so he could not remove the key.

c) He knew that he would be returning shortly to bring some tea to Mr. Soames.

d) He had arranged with Gilchrist that he would leave the key in the door.

D Mark T for true or F for false.

❶ Mr. Soames lived at St. Luke's College. T F

❷ Mr. Soames was a young man. T F

❸ Mr. Soames was a professor. T F

A Clue Made of Clay

The next morning, Holmes came to me at breakfast time.

"I have been up for two hours, gathering evidence," he said.

"I believe that I have solved the mystery."

He held out his hand.

Three little pyramids of black clay sat in his palm.

"You only had two yesterday," I said.

"Where did the third come from?"

"I'll tell you when we get to the college," he said.

KEY WORDS

- clue
- made of
- be up
- gather
- evidence

- believe
- hold out (hold-held-held)
- palm
- come from
- get to

- be eager to + *Verb*
- what one has to say
- make a suggestion
- turn white
- even

When we arrived at the college, Mr. Soames was eager to hear what Holmes had to say.

"Please call Bannister," said Holmes.

When Bannister arrived, Holmes made some suggestions about what had happened.

As he listened, Bannister turned even whiter than before.

"I think that you sat in the chair by the window to hide something," said Holmes.

"As soon as Mr. Soames had gone, you released the man who was hiding in the bedroom.

That man was Gilchrist."

I gasped. How did Sherlock Holmes know that?

Mr. Soames hurried away.

He returned almost at once with Gilchrist.

The student was unusually tall and agile with a pleasant face and blue eyes.

When he realized that he had been discovered, he fell onto his knees, sobbing.

Sherlock Holmes explained how he had solved the mystery.

KEY WORDS

- **hide** (hide-hid-hidden)
- **release**
- **gasp**
- **hurry away**
- **unusually**
- **agile**
- **pleasant**
- **realize**
- **fall onto one's knees** (fall-fell-fallen)

- **sob**
- **explain**
- **as** + *Positive Adjective/Adverb* + as
- **be able to** + *Verb*
- **notice**
- **decide**
- **panic** (*cf*. panicked)
- **snatch up**
- **let ~ out**

"When I looked through the window from the outside,
I realized that only a man as tall as Gilchrist would be
able to see through it to the desk inside.
Only he would be able to see that there was an exam on
the desk.
When he noticed the key in the door, he decided to go in
and look at the exam.
When Mr. Soames returned, Gilchrist panicked.
He snatched up his shoes and hid in the bedroom.
There he stayed until Mr. Soames left to come and find
me.
Then, when all was quiet, Bannister let him out."

How did Holmes know all this?

He went on to explain.

"This morning, before breakfast, I went to the fields
where the long jump takes place.

I took some of the black clay from the long jump pit."

He held out a pyramid in his hand.

"This must have got stuck to the spikes on Gilchrist's running shoes. 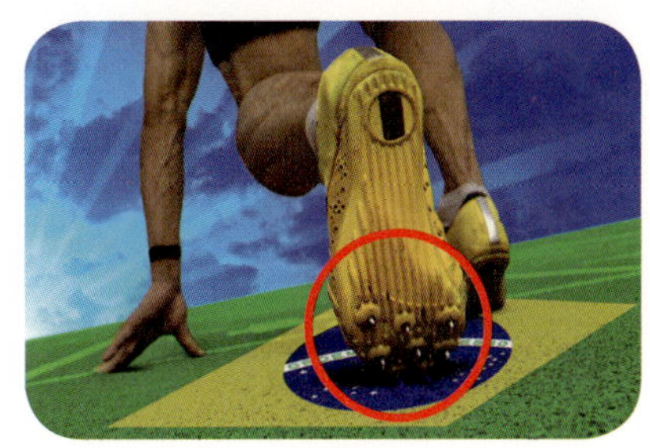

▲ spikes

He was probably carrying them when he came in here. He put them down on the writing table.

The clay fell off and the spikes scratched the table.

The scratch on the table is deeper on the side that is close to the bedroom door.

That tells us that Gilchrist snatched up his spiked shoes. He dragged them across the table as he ran to the bedroom to hide.

That is why there was some clay in the bedroom, too.

When Bannister came in, he saw something belonging to Gilchrist on the chair...."

KEY WORDS

- field
- pit
- get stuck
- spike
- running shoes
- probably
- carry
- put down
- fall off
- scratch
- drag

"His gloves," said Bannister.

"He left his gloves there and I recognized them.

I have known Gilchrist since he was a child.

I am a friend of his father's.

I sat on the chair to hide them, and I did let Gilchrist out

of the bedroom when nobody was looking."

Gilchrist was very sorry about what he had done.

He declared that he would not take the exam.

He had decided to travel overseas and become a

policeman.

Now it all made sense.

Sherlock Holmes had solved the mystery once again.

Comprehension Quiz

A According to the story, choose the right verb for the blank to complete each sentence.

| turned | released | solved | recognized |

❶ I believe that I have ________________ the mystery.

❷ Bannister ________________ even whiter than before.

❸ You ________________ the man who was hiding in the bedroom.

❹ I ________________ his gloves.

B Put the sentences in order.

❶ Gilchrist snatched up his shoes.

❷ Gilchrist noticed the key in the door.

❸ Gilchrist read the exam.

❹ Gilchrist hid in the bedroom.

________ → ________ → ________ → ________

  Choose the best answer to each question.

❶ What evidence did Sherlock Holmes gather in order to solve the mystery?

a) He measured the height of all the students.

b) He found a pair of gloves.

c) He found the third pyramid of black clay.

d) He looked at the handwriting of all the students.

❷ Why did Bannister sit in the chair nearest the window?

a) He wanted to look at the view outside the window.

b) He wanted to hide Gilchrist's gloves, which were on the chair.

c) He wanted to stay there and tell Mr. Soames about Gilchrist.

d) He felt faint and it was the nearest chair to him when he wanted to sit down.

❸ What did Gilchrist plan to do next? Choose *two* answers.

a) He planned to go to a different college.

b) He planned to study a different subject.

c) He planned to go overseas.

d) He planned to become a policeman.

The Adventure of the
Red-Headed League

Chapter One

A Strange Kind of Work

One day in the fall, I called upon my friend, Sherlock Holmes.

When I arrived, I found that he already had a visitor.

He was a large man with fiery red hair.

"This is Mr. Wilson," said Holmes.

"He has come to report something unusual."

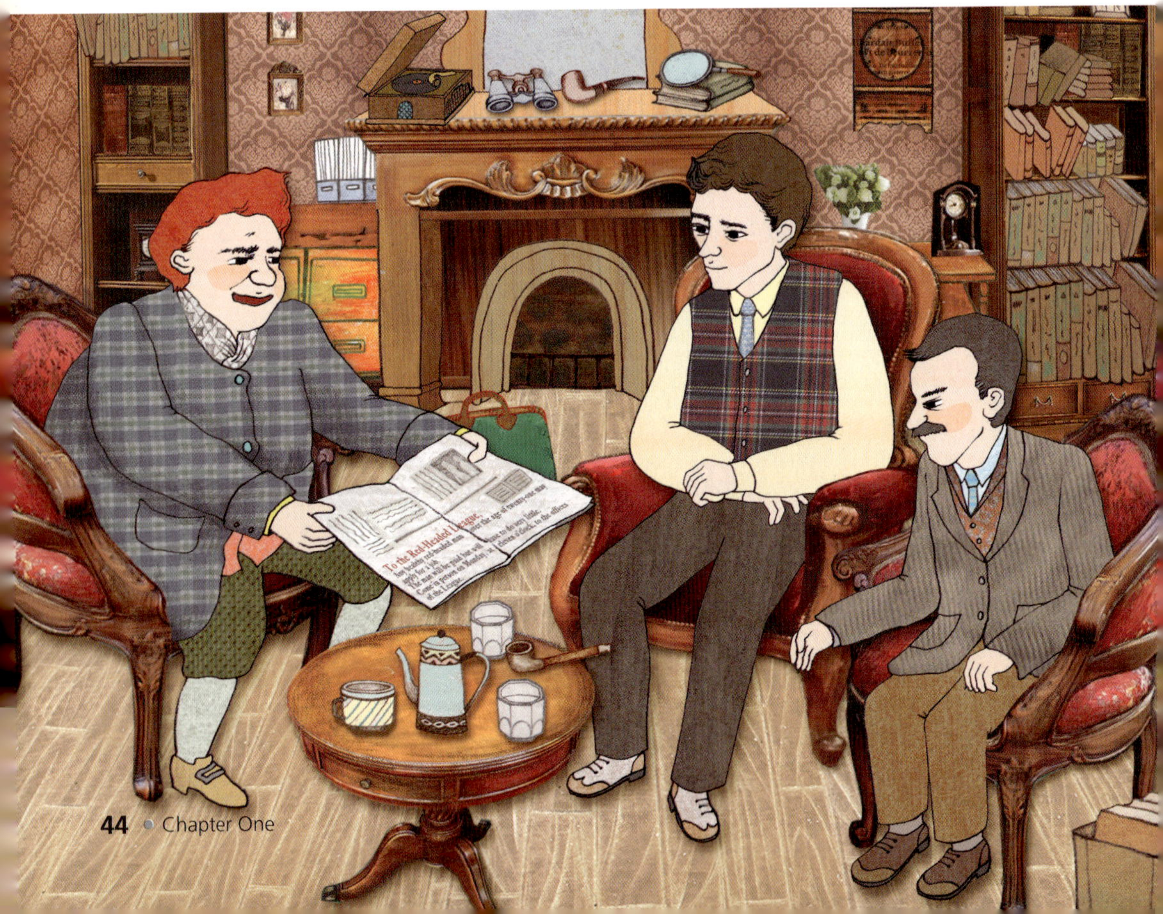

Mr. Wilson pulled out a newspaper from the inside pocket of his coat.

He leaned forward to show us an advertisement in the newspaper.

To the Red-Headed League, it said.

Any healthy red-headed man over the age of twenty-one may apply for a job.

The man will be paid but will have to do very little.

Come in person on Monday, at eleven o'clock, to the office of the League.

The newspaper had been published two months earlier.

POP QUIZ

What did Mr. Wilson pull out from the inside pocket of his coat?

ⓐ a gun
ⓑ a newspaper

Mr. Wilson settled back in his chair to tell us his story.

"I have a small shop," he began, "but I don't make much money.

I have one assistant, called Vincent Spaulding.

He works for half the usual wages.

He's very intelligent.

He takes photographs of everything.

He spends a lot of time in the cellar.

He develops his photographs there in the dark.

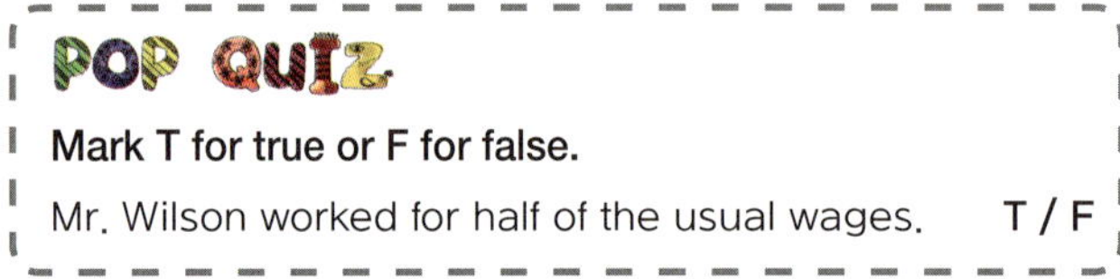

KEY WORDS

- settle back
- make money
- assistant
- usual (↔ unusual)
- wage
- intelligent
- take a photograph of
- cellar
- develop
- dark
- certain
- shade
- pale
- address
- push (↔ pull)
- crowd

It was Spaulding who first showed me this
advertisement.

He told me that only a certain shade of red hair would
do.

Not too pale, not too dark, but fiery red like mine.

He went with me to the address given.

Every red-haired man in London was there as well!

Spaulding pushed and pulled me through the crowd."

"We reached the steps that led up to the office," he went on.

"Some men were already coming out. They looked disappointed.

Inside, there was an office. It was empty but for two wooden chairs and a table.

Behind the table sat a short man with red hair.

But as soon as he saw me, he declared that I was perfect for the job.

The hours of work were between 10 a.m. and 2 p.m. each day.

Spaulding kindly said that he would look after my shop while I was away.

But the work was very strange.

I had to go to the office every day and copy out information from an encyclopedia.

I was not allowed to leave the building at all during those hours.

Each day, I copied another section from the encyclopedia.

At the end of each week, I received my pay."

KEY WORDS

- reach
- steps
- look + *Adjective*
- disappointed
- empty
- but for + *Noun*
- behind

- perfect for (*cf.* perfect)
- look after
- copy out
- encyclopedia
- be allowed to + *Verb*
- not ~ at all
- section

"This morning, after eight weeks of work, everything suddenly came to an end, " he sighed.

"When I went to work, the door was locked. A notice was nailed to it."

▲ cardboard

Mr. Wilson handed us the cardboard notice.

It said: *The Red-Headed League is dissolved. October 9, 1890.*

"What did you do when you found the notice?" asked Holmes.

How long did Mr. Wilson work for the Red-Headed League?

ⓐ eight weeks
ⓑ eight months

KEY WORDS

- suddenly
- come to an end
- sigh
- nail

- cardboard
- dissolve
- ask around
- hear of

- by mail
- good enough

"I asked around if anyone knew about the Red-Headed
League. Nobody had heard of it.

I went back to my shop, and asked Spaulding what he
thought.

He said that perhaps I would hear something by mail.

But that is not good enough, Mr. Holmes.

I have heard that you give good advice, which is why I
have come to see you."

Holmes asked Mr. Wilson several questions about
Vincent Spaulding.

It seemed that he was a short man. 

His ears were pierced for earrings.

He had a white mark upon his forehead.

After answering these questions, our visitor left us.

Holmes sat in his chair, smoking his pipe, and thought.

Suddenly, he leaped out of his chair.

"Will you come with me to a concert of German music
this afternoon, Dr. Watson?" he asked.

I was not busy, so I agreed to go.

What kind of music did Sherlock Holmes want to go and listen to?

ⓐ German music
ⓑ French music

KEY WORDS

- pierce
- earring
- forehead
- pipe
- leap
- agree

Comprehension Quiz

A Complete the details of the job advertisement appearing in the story.

❶ Hair color of the man: _______________

❷ Age of the man: over _______________

❸ Day the man must come: _______________

❹ Time the man must come: _______________

B Fill in each blank with the right word below.

fiery	disappointed	perfect	short

❶ Any man who wanted the job had to have _______________ red hair.

❷ Behind the table sat a _______________ man with red hair.

❸ The men coming out looked _______________.

❹ The red-haired man declared that Mr. Wilson was _______________ for the job.

C Choose the best answer to each question.

❶ In what season did this case take place?

a) spring   b) summer

c) fall   d) winter

❷ What did Spaulding say that he would do while Mr. Wilson was away?

a) read the newspaper

b) develop photographs

c) look after the shop

d) copy out information from an encyclopedia

D Mark T for true or F for false.

❶ Vincent Spaulding worked for twice the usual wages.   T F

❷ Vincent Spaulding was not very intelligent.   T F

❸ Vincent Spaulding took photographs of everything.   T F

❹ Vincent Spaulding spent a lot of time in the cellar.   T F

Underground Secrets

On the way to the concert, we passed Mr. Wilson's shop.

Holmes stopped in front of the shop.

He thumped on the pavement three times with his walking stick.

Then, he went up to the door and knocked.

A young man opened the door. He had a white mark on his forehead.

His ears were pierced for earrings.

I guessed that he must be Vincent Spaulding.

Holmes asked him for directions. Spaulding gave them, then went back inside and shut the door.

KEY WORDS

- underground
- on the way to
- pass
- in front of
- thump
- pavement
- walking stick
- guess
- direction
- shut (shut-shut-shut)
- trousers
- strike (strike-struck-stricken/struck)
- explore
- busy street
- as though (= as if)

"Why did you ask for directions?" I asked Holmes.

"You know where we are."

"I wanted to see the knees of his trousers," he replied.

"And why did you strike the pavement with your stick?"
I asked.

Sherlock Holmes did not answer. Instead, he took me
with him to explore the busy road behind the shop.
He looked at all the shops and buildings along that busy
street.

We then continued to the concert. Holmes enjoyed the
music as though he had nothing else to think about.

When we came out, Holmes said, "I believe that a serious crime is about to be committed.

I shall need your help tonight. It may be dangerous, so bring your gun."

I did not understand what was going on, but I went to meet him that evening at his house on Baker Street.

When I got there, he was talking to a police officer called Peter Jones.

Another man was there — Mr. Merryweather, who was the director of a bank.

They were after a well-known thief called John Clay.

I did not know how this was connected with the mystery that we were investigating.

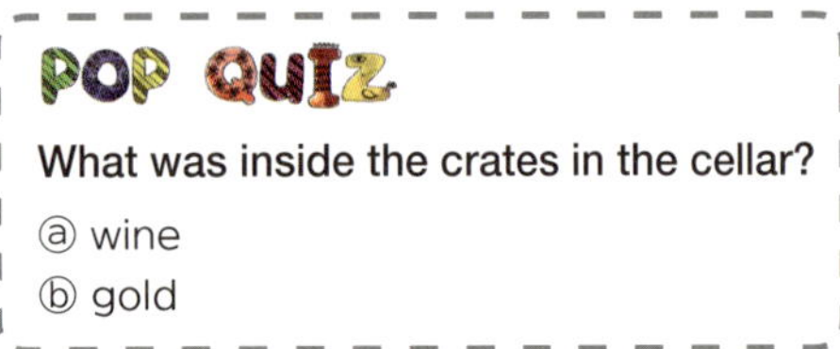

KEY WORDS

- serious
- crime
- be about to + *Verb*
- commit
- shall + *Verb*
- director
- be after

- well-known
- thief
- be connected with
- investigate
- passage
- damp
- earth

- underneath
- be piled with
- crate
- steal (steal-stole-stolen)
- put out

We went to the busy road behind Mr. Wilson's shop.

There, Mr. Merryweather took us through a door in the wall of a building.

We went down some steps into a dark passage.

It smelled of damp earth.

We arrived at a cellar underneath Mr. Merryweather's bank. It was piled with boxes and crates.

"There is gold inside the crates," said Mr. Merryweather.

"We believe that John Clay wants to steal it."

Holmes put out the lamp and we sat in the dark, waiting to see who might arrive.

We waited and waited.

At last, I saw a line of light coming from the floor as someone lifted one of the stone slabs.

A white hand appeared, followed by a face.

A youngish man climbed out of the hole.

It was Vincent Spaulding, followed by a red-haired companion.

"It's all clear," whispered Spaulding.

But Holmes leaped out. He grabbed Spaulding by the collar.

The red-haired man dived back down the hole.

Mr. Jones tried to grab him, but there was a tearing sound. The man escaped.

But he left behind part of his coat in Mr. Jones' hand.

"It doesn't matter," said Holmes.

"He may escape back down this tunnel.

But there are three policemen waiting for him at the other end."

John Clay and Vincent Spaulding were the same person.
Holmes explained the whole story to me.
"The Red-Headed League was a plan to get Mr. Wilson
out of his shop for a few hours each day," he said.
"It was a strange way to do it, but it worked very well.
Vincent Spaulding worked for very low wages.
I knew that he must have another reason for wanting to
be at the shop.
When I heard that he spent a lot of time in the cellar,
I was suspicious.
I guessed that he must be digging a tunnel.

I beat upon the pavement with my stick. That is because
I was listening for a hollow sound under the pavement.
In this way, I worked out in which direction the tunnel
went.
When Spaulding opened the door, the knees of his
trousers were wrinkled and stained.
It looked as though he had been on his knees, digging."

KEY WORDS

- whole
- suspicious
- **dig** (dig-dug-dug)
- **beat** (beat-beat-beaten)
- listen for
- hollow
- work out
- wrinkle
- stain

"I walked around the corner and saw that a bank was
on the road behind Mr. Wilson's shop," Holmes went on.

"It was near the shop.

At once, the mystery was solved!

I guessed that Spaulding wanted to rob the bank.

He was digging a tunnel from Mr. Wilson's cellar to the
bank's cellar.

That is why he spent so much time down there."

I shook my head in wonder.

"You solve these mysteries so well!" I said.

Holmes yawned.

"Thinking about them saves me from boredom," he
said.

"But I hope my skill is useful to someone."

KEY WORDS

- rob
- **shake** (shake-shook-shaken)
- in wonder
- yawn

- save
- boredom
- skill
- useful

POP QUIZ

Where was the bank?

ⓐ on the road behind Mr. Wilson's shop
ⓑ in the tunnel next to Mr. Wilson's cellar

Comprehension Quiz

A Find the explanation about each character to correctly complete each sentence.

❶ Mr. Merryweather •   • a) was a police officer.

❷ John Clay •   • b) owned a shop close to the bank.

❸ Peter Jones •   • c) was the director of a bank.

❹ Mr. Wilson •   • d) was a well-known thief.

B Put the sentences in order.

❶ Holmes knocked on the door.

❷ Holmes looked at all the shops and buildings along the street.

❸ Holmes asked Spaulding for directions.

❹ Holmes thumped on the pavement with his walking stick.

_______ → _______ → _______ → _______

C Choose the best answer to each question.

❶ Why did Vincent Spaulding spend so much time in the cellar of Mr. Wilson's shop?

a) He was developing his photographs.

b) He was allergic to sunlight.

c) He was making a storeroom.

d) He was digging a tunnel.

❷ Why did a line of light shine through the floor?

a) Sherlock Holmes switched on the lamp.

b) Dr. Watson lit a match.

c) Vincent Spaulding lifted a stone slab off of the floor.

d) Peter Jones shone a flashlight.

❸ Why did the Red-Headed League exist?

a) to help people with red hair

b) to write new encyclopedias

c) to get Mr. Wilson out of his shop every day

d) to provide jobs for people

The Adventure of the
Six Napoleons

Burglaries and Broken Busts

The police inspector,
Mr. Lestrade, often visited
Sherlock Holmes.
He always had interesting
information for us.
One evening, he arrived
with an unusual story to tell.
"It began four days ago," he said,
"at Morse Hudson's shop."
I knew the shop. It sold pictures and statues.

KEY WORDS

- **Napoleon** (Napoléon Bonaparte)
- burglary
- broken
- bust
- **police inspector** (*cf.* inspector)
- statue
- for a moment
- crash
- plaster
- smash
- to pieces
- rush
- see if
- no sign of

"The shop assistant left the shop for a moment," said
Mr. Lestrade.

"He heard a crash and hurried back at once.

Someone had taken a bust of Napoleon, made of plaster,

and had smashed it to pieces.

The shop assistant rushed outside to see if anyone was

in the street.

Some people had seen a man running out of the shop.

But there was no sign of him now."

▲ a statue of Napoleon

▲ a bust of Napoleon

"How strange," I said.

"Yes, and you will think it even stranger when I tell
you that the same thing happened again last night,"
Mr. Lestrade went on.

"In the same road as Morse Hudson's shop, there is a
doctor's house.

A man called Dr. Barnicot lives there. He sees some
patients there.

He also has his doctor's office about two miles away.

Dr. Barnicot bought two Napoleon busts from Morse
Hudson's shop. They were identical.

One of them was in his house. The other was at his
office.

This morning, when he came down to breakfast, he
found that his house had been robbed.

Nothing had been taken except the bust of Napoleon.

He found it outside in the garden, smashed to pieces."

POP QUIZ

Who lived on the same road as Morse Hudson's shop?

ⓐ Dr. Barnicot   ⓑ Dr. Watson

KEY WORDS

- patient
- doctor's office
- mile (1mile = 1,609m)
- identical
- except

Holmes rubbed his hands together. He loved a good mystery to think about.

"This is certainly unusual," he said.

"But I haven't finished yet," said Mr. Lestrade.

"When Dr. Barnicot went to his office at twelve o'clock, he found that someone had broken in. They had smashed the second bust to pieces as well."

We had many questions to think about as we went to bed.

KEY WORDS

- rub one's hands (together)
- certainly
- yet
- break in (break-broke-broken)
- message

Next morning, before breakfast, Holmes received a
message from Mr. Lestrade.

"He wants us to meet him at once," he said. "Something
else has happened."

We hurried to the address given in the message.

It was on Pitt Street, in the area of London called
Kensington. A crowd had gathered outside number 31.

When we arrived at the front door, we saw Mr. Lestrade's
face at the window.

We hurried inside to meet him.

The owner of the house was an old man called
Mr. Horace Harker. He worked for a newspaper.
Now he was pacing up and down in his dressing gown.
He looked very worried.
"Four months ago," he began, "I bought a bust of
Napoleon from Harding Brothers.
I put it here, in my house, and thought no more about it.
As a journalist, I often work at night, so I was awake
and working at three o'clock this morning.
I heard some strange sounds. Then, there was
a dreadful yell from outside.
I rushed into this room and saw at once that
the bust had gone.
The window was wide open.

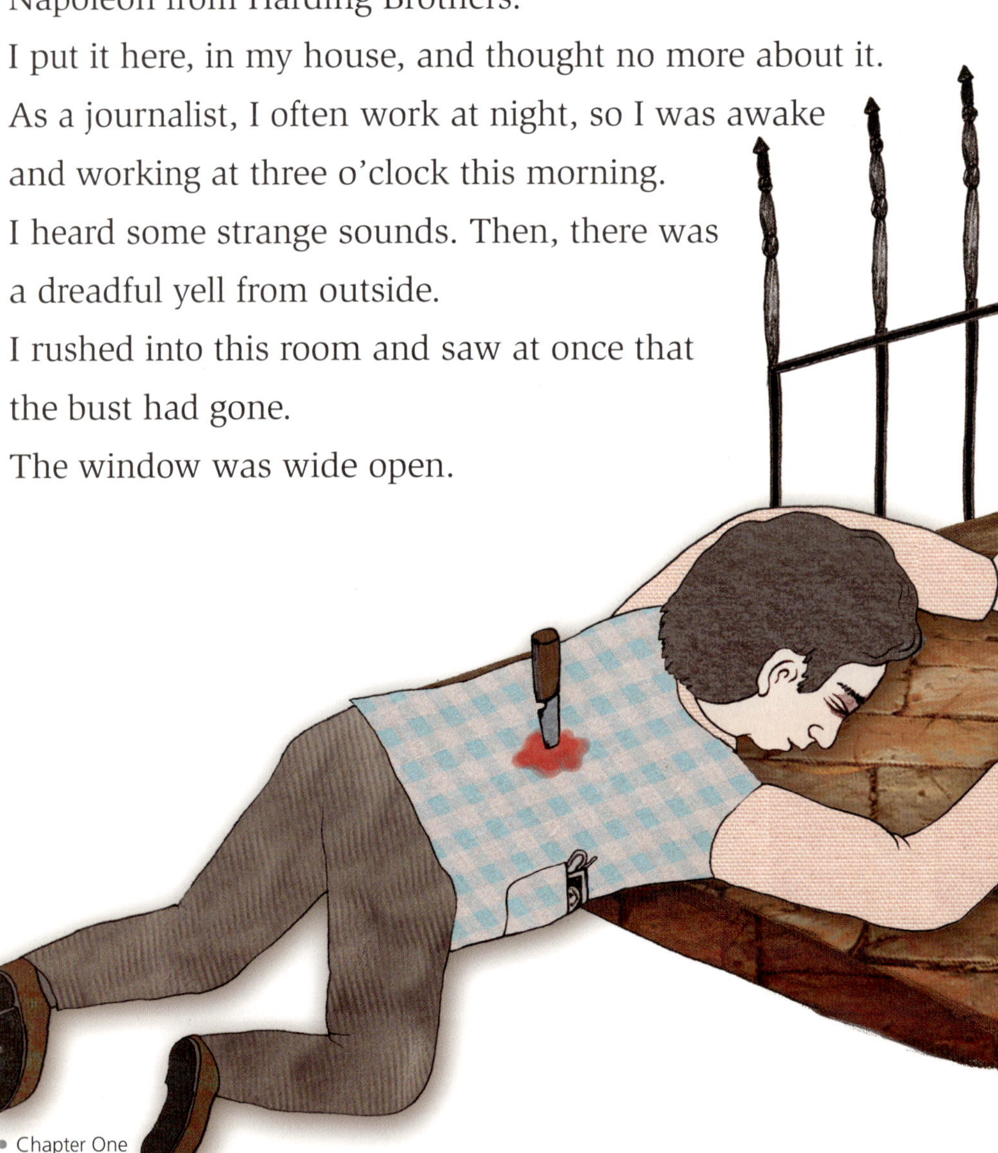

I think the burglar stepped from the window to the front door steps.

But there must have been someone else there, too.

When I opened the front door, I found a dead man!

He had been stabbed with a knife."

KEY WORDS

- owner
- pace up and down
- dressing gown
- journalist
- dreadful
- yell
- wide open
- burglar
- stab

"Who was the dead man?"
Holmes asked Mr. Lestrade.
"We don't know," said Mr.
Lestrade.
"He was tall, with skin
darkened by the sun.
In his pockets were an apple,
some string, a map of London,
and a photograph."

Mr. Lestrade held out the photograph to show us.
It showed a short man with thick eyebrows.
He looked rather like a gorilla.
"Has the bust been found?" asked Holmes.
Mr. Lestrade nodded. "It was found outside an empty
house in the next street.
It had been smashed to pieces, just like the others."
Holmes wanted to see the place where the bust had
been found.
Mr. Lestrade and I went with him to have a look.

• darkened by	• eyebrow	• ground
• string	• look like	• choose (choose-chose-chosen)
• thick	• have a look	• shrug

He picked up several of the pieces from the ground and studied them.

"Why was the bust carried here?" he asked.

"Why wasn't it broken near Mr. Harker's house?"

"This is an empty house," said Mr. Lestrade.

"He could break it here without disturbing anyone."

"Yes, but there is another empty house closer to

Mr. Harker's," said Holmes.

"Why did he choose this one?"

Mr. Lestrade shrugged. "I don't know."

Holmes pointed to the street lamp above our heads.

"I think he brought it here because he could see what he was doing.

There is no street lamp outside the other empty house."

Mr. Lestrade agreed that this may be true.

"I will go and try to discover the identity of the dead man," he announced, and away he went.

- street lamp
- identity
- announce
- sculpture
- works
- originally
- pour
- mold
- dry
- harden

Holmes and I went to the sculpture works where the
busts were originally made.

The manager told us that six identical Napoleon busts
had been made over a year ago.

Three had been sent to Morse Hudson. Three had been
sent to Harding Brothers in Kensington.

He showed us how the busts were made.

Soft plaster was poured into the molds and then left to
dry and harden.

"Do you know this man?" Holmes showed him the photograph.

The manager's face went red with anger.

"Yes, I do know him. He's called Beppo.

He worked here over a year ago.

He injured another Italian man in the street, using a knife.

The police came here and arrested him. He went to prison for a year, so he is probably out now."

Next, we went to Harding Brothers. Mr. Harker had bought his bust of Napoleon from there.

"We had three of those busts," said Mr. Harding. "The other two were sold to Mr. Brown of Chiswick and Mr. Sandeford of Reading."

After our meeting with Mr. Harding, we went to visit Mr. Lestrade once more.

"I have discovered the identity of the dead man!" he exclaimed.

"His name is Pietro Venucci, an Italian man and a known criminal."

I did not recognize the name, but Holmes seemed pleased to hear it.

"If you will both come with me to Chiswick tonight, then I think we will catch our man," he said.

POP QUIZ

Who was the dead man?
ⓐ a known criminal
ⓑ a manager of the sculpture works

KEY WORDS

- go red with anger
- injure
- arrest
- prison
- exclaim
- known
- criminal

Comprehension Quiz

Chapter One

 **A** Circle the character who spoke each line.

❶ "Why was the bust carried here?"

MR. LESTRADE / SHERLOCK HOLMES

❷ "He could break it here without disturbing anyone."

MR. LESTRADE / SHERLOCK HOLMES

❸ "Why did he choose this one?"

MR. LESTRADE / SHERLOCK HOLMES

❹ "I will go and try to discover the identity of the dead man."

MR. LESTRADE / SHERLOCK HOLMES

B Mark T for true or F for false.

❶ The shop assistant had smashed a bust of Napoleon.   T   F

❷ The shop assistant left the shop for an hour.   T   F

❸ The shop assistant heard a crash.   T   F

❹ The shop assistant saw a man running out of the shop.   T   F

  Choose the best answer to each question.

❶ Where was the bust from Dr. Barnicot's house found?

a) in the garden

b) under a street lamp

c) in the kitchen

d) on the front steps

❷ What did Sherlock Holmes receive before breakfast?

a) a visitor   b) a message

c) a parcel   d) a clue

D Put the sentences in order.

❶ Mr. Harker saw a dead man on the steps outside his house.

❷ Mr. Harker rushed into the room where the bust was kept.

❸ Mr. Harker heard some strange sounds.

❹ Mr. Harker opened the front door.

________ → ________ → ________ → ________

A Hidden Pearl

That night, we went to the house of Mr. Brown in
Chiswick.

Everything was quiet.

We hid in the shadows by the garden fence, and waited.

Before long, someone appeared.

It was a man, as quick and active as an ape.

He hurried up the garden path and opened a window.

KEY WORDS

- hidden
- pearl
- before long
- active
- ape
- path
- flash
- shortly afterward
- turn away from (*cf.* turn)
- crouch
- sharp
- tap
- rattling
- **creep** (creep-crept-crept)
- up behind
- grab hold of

Suddenly, there was the flash of a lamp inside a dark
room. The man was inside the house!

Shortly afterward, he came out again, carrying
something white under his arm.

He turned away from us and crouched down.

There was a sharp tap, followed by a rattling sound.

We crept up behind him and grabbed hold of him.

A moment later, Mr. Lestrade had the handcuffs on him.

He turned his face towards us.

I saw that it was Beppo, the man in the photograph.

But now that Beppo was caught, Holmes did not seem interested in him.

Instead, he bent over the white object.

It was another bust of Napoleon, smashed to pieces like the others.

"Are you going to explain everything, Holmes?" asked Mr. Lestrade.

"Not yet," said Holmes.

"There are one or two more things I need to do.

Come and see me tomorrow evening. I will explain everything then."

KEY WORDS

- **handcuffs** (*cf.* handcuff)
- **towards**
- **bend** (bend-bent-bent)
- **object**

POP QUIZ
What did Holmes do after Beppo was caught?
ⓐ He explained everything.
ⓑ He bent over the white object.

When we met the next evening, we were disturbed by a knock at the door.

An old man came into the room where we were sitting.

He placed a large bag on the table. Holmes greeted him.

"Are you Mr. Sandeford, of Reading?"

"Yes, I am," said the man.

"I was surprised to get your letter saying that you wanted to buy my bust of Napoleon.

You agreed to pay me ten pounds, so I have brought you the bust."

KEY WORDS

- place
- greet
- destroy

- to one's surprise
- sharply
- break into pieces

- triumph
- sphere

He took from his bag a white plaster bust of Napoleon.

It was identical to the other five that Beppo had destroyed.

Holmes paid Mr. Sandeford, who took the money and left.

To my surprise, Holmes then placed the bust on a clean white cloth.

He struck it sharply on top of the head.

It broke into pieces.

With a cry of triumph, Sherlock Holmes picked up a small, black sphere.

"It is the famous black pearl of the Borgias!" Holmes
cried.

"But that disappeared just over a year ago," said Mr.
Lestrade.

"It was stolen from a princess by her Italian maid,
Lucretia Venucci."

"Yes," agreed Holmes. "Her brother was the dead man
on Mr. Harker's front door step, Pietro Venucci.
As soon as I heard his name, I knew that the pearl was
involved in this case.

He and Beppo knew each other.
Venucci had the pearl.
He got it from his sister.
Beppo injured Venucci in the
street last year and took the
pearl for himself.

When the police came to the sculpture works to arrest
him, Beppo knew that he had to hide the pearl.
He pressed it into the soft plaster of one of the Napoleon
busts as it was drying.
Then, he smoothed over the surface so that nobody
would know."

POP QUIZ

Choose the right word for the underlined part.
First, (Venucci / Beppo) had the pearl.
Then (Venucci / Beppo) injured (Venucci / Beppo) and
took the pearl for himself.

KEY WORDS

- maid
- be involved in

- for oneself
- press

- smooth
- surface

"Beppo went to prison for a year," Holmes went on.

"During that time, the six busts were sold to different people.

When he came out of prison, Beppo went looking for those busts.

He smashed each one to pieces, hoping to find the one in which the pearl was hidden.

And here it is, in my hand."

Mr. Lestrade looked at him in admiration.

But Sherlock Holmes was already thinking about the next mystery.

"Put the pearl in the safe, Watson," he said.

"Take out the papers concerning our next case."

Comprehension Quiz

A  Match each character and his or her job to correctly complete each sentence.

❶ Mr. Lestrade was a   •

❷ Morse Hudson was a   •

❸ Horace Harker was a   •

❹ Pietro Venucci was a   •

    • a) journalist.

    • b) shop owner.

    • c) criminal.

    • d) police inspector.

B  Circle the right word for each underlined part.

❶ Beppo had worked at the sculpture works one (<u>week / month / year</u>) earlier.

❷ Beppo had injured another Italian man in the (<u>street / shop / surgery</u>).

❸ Beppo had used a (<u>bust / brick / knife</u>) to injure the other man.

❹ Beppo had been sent to (<u>Italy / prison / hospital</u>) for a while.

C Choose the best answer to each question.

❶ How did the ape-like man get into the house?

a) He knocked on the door and someone let him in.

b) He unlocked the door with a key.

c) He opened a window and climbed in.

d) He broke a window and climbed in.

❷ Who did the black pearl originally belong to?

a) Beppo

b) a princess

c) Pietro Venucci

d) Lucretia Venucci

❸ Where did Beppo hide the pearl?

a) He gave it to Pietro Venucci to look after.

b) He buried it in a secret location.

c) He pressed it into the soft plaster of one of the Napoleon busts.

d) He took it to prison and hid it there.

Fill in the blanks to review the story.

Stories of ____________

Case 1: The Adventure of the ____________
- Mystery: Who entered the rooms of Mr. Soames and read the e________ ?
- Clues: a) Two pyramids of black c________ were found.
    b) The leather covering of the w________ had a cut in it.
- Solution: A student, Gilchrist, read the e________ .
    The c________ pyramids were from the long j________ pit.
    The cut was from the s________ of his running shoes.

Case 2: The Adventure of the ____________
- Mystery: Why was Mr. Wilson paid to sit in a room and copy from an e________ ?
- Clues: a) Vincent Spaulding spent a lot of time in the c________ beneath Mr. Wilson's s________ .
    b) There was a hollow sound beneath the p________ near Mr. Wilson's shop.
- Solution: V________ Spaulding was digging a t________ to rob the bank.
    He and his friend invented the job for Mr. W________ to get him out of the way.

Case 3: The Adventure of the ____________
- Mystery: Why was someone stealing b________ of Napoleon and smashing them to pieces?
- Clues: a) A dead man was found with a p________ of an ape-like man in his pocket.
    b) One of the b________ was broken beneath a street lamp.
- Solution: B________ had hidden a valuable p________ in one of the busts.
    He was breaking them open to find the p________ .

Let's Think & Talk

Think about the following questions and answer them freely.

❶ Among the three stories, which one do you think the most interesting? Why?

❷ In the three stories, did you figure out who the culprit is before Sherlock Holmes did? Based on what did you guess he or she was the culprit? If you didn't guess right, what made it hard for you to guess who the culprit is?

❸ Among the three stories, choose one and rewrite it. What if there had been a trap that even Sherlock Holmes hadn't noticed? What if Sherlock Holmes hadn't found the culprit but instead had accused the wrong person? Use your imagination and create your own story that is even more interesting.

❹ Among Sir Conan Doyle's mystery stories, do you know any other stories besides the ones in this book? Tell us the plot.

Let's Review the Story

Stories of Sherlock Holmes

Case 1: The Adventure of the Three Students

- Mystery: Who entered the rooms of Mr. Soames and read the exam ?
- Clues: a) Two pyramids of black clay were found.
    b) The leather covering of the writing desk had a cut in it.
- Solution: A student, Gilchrist, read the exam .
    The clay pyramids were from the long jump pit.
    The cut was from the spikes of his running shoes.

Case 2: The Adventure of the Red-Headed League

- Mystery: Why was Mr. Wilson paid to sit in a room and copy from an encylopedia ?
- Clues: a) Vincent Spaulding spent a lot of time in the cellar beneath Mr. Wilson's shop .
    b) There was a hollow sound beneath the pavement near Mr. Wilson's shop.
- Solution: Vincent Spaulding was digging a tunnel to rob the bank.
    He and his friend invented the job for Mr. Wilson to get him out of the way.

Case 3: The Adventure of the Six Napoleons

- Mystery: Why was someone stealing busts of Napoleon and smashing them to pieces?
- Clues: a) A dead man was found with a photograph of an ape-like man in his pocket.
    b) One of the busts was broken beneath a street lamp.
- Solution: Beppo had hidden a valuable pearl in one of the busts.
    He was breaking them open to find the pearl .

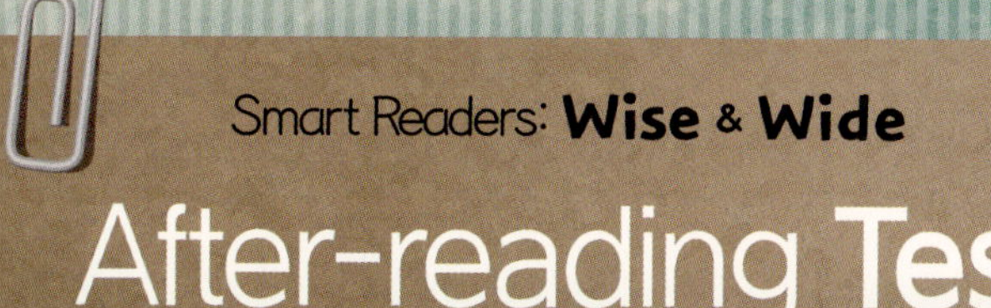

- Stories of Sherlock Holmes
- Level 4
- 30 Questions

(Vocabulary 7 / Reading Comprehension 16 /

Sentence Structure & Grammar 7)

1. What does "agile" mean in the following sentence?

   Gilchrist was <u>agile</u>.

   ① handsome　　　　　　　　② intelligent
   ③ thin　　　　　　　　　　④ athletic

2. What does "identical" mean in the following sentence?

   Dr. Barnicot bought two Napoleon busts, which were <u>identical</u>.

   ① expensive　　　　　　　　② historical
   ③ exactly the same　　　　　④ stolen

3. Which of the following has the wrong past tense form of the verb?
   ① lie − lay　　　　　　　　② sit − sat
   ③ put − put　　　　　　　　④ stand − stand

4. What is the common word for the two blanks?

   - Now it all ___________ sense.
   - When Bannister arrived, Holmes ___________ some suggestions about what had happened.

   ① made　　　　　　　　　　② did
   ③ understood　　　　　　　④ gave

※ Choose the right word for each blank. (5~6)

5.
   He is very good ___________ the long jump.

   ① of　　　　　　　　　　　② at
   ③ to　　　　　　　　　　　④ along

6.

> Thinking about them ___________ me from boredom.

① saves   ② gives
③ makes   ④ has

7. Which "since" has a different meaning from the others?
   ① <u>Since</u> I was late to school again, I deserved punishment.
   ② He must have recovered, <u>since</u> he is no longer here.
   ③ <u>Since</u> I was very tired, I went to bed early.
   ④ I've lived in Seoul <u>since</u> I was eight.

8. Who narrates *The Adventure of the Three Students*?
   ① Sherlock Holmes
   ② Dr. Watson
   ③ Mr. Soames
   ④ Bannister

9. What had happened to Mr. Soames' new writing table?
   ① Someone had turned it over.
   ② Someone had spilled ink on it.
   ③ Someone had moved it into the bedroom.
   ④ Someone had made a cut in its leather surface.

10. How did Holmes know that the intruder had been in the bedroom?
    ① There were footprints on the carpet.
    ② There was someone hiding behind the curtains.
    ③ There was a pyramid of black clay on the floor.
    ④ There was a page of the exam on the bed.

11. What did Gilchrist do when his crime was discovered? Choose *two* answers.
   ① He started to sob.
   ② He denied that he had done it.
   ③ He said that he would not take the exam.
   ④ He blamed it all on Bannister.

12. Where did the black clay come from?
   ① the college garden
   ② the river bed
   ③ the long jump pit
   ④ the local park

13. Which of these is NOT a description of Vincent Spaulding?
   ① He was a short man.
   ② He had ears that were pierced.
   ③ He had a white mark on his forehead.
   ④ He had red hair.

14. Where did the dark passage Mr. Holmes went down lead to?
   ① a cellar beneath the concert hall
   ② a cellar beneath the bank
   ③ a cellar beneath Mr. Wilson's shop
   ④ a cellar beneath Holmes' house

15. Why did Sherlock Holmes beat on the pavement with his stick?
   ① to see if it was hollow underneath
   ② to frighten anyone who may be digging below
   ③ to see if his stick was strong
   ④ to call Vincent Spaulding to open the door

16. Why did Vincent Spaulding work for such low wages?
　① He was rich and did not need the money.
　② He had another job that paid highly.
　③ He made money from his photography.
　④ He just wanted a reason to be at Mr. Wilson's shop all the time.

17. Why were the knees of Vincent Spaulding's trousers wrinkled and stained?
　① He had been cleaning the floor in the shop.
　② He had been gardening behind the shop.
　③ He had been digging a tunnel beneath the shop.
　④ He had been inspecting the pavement in front of the shop.

18. Who or what did Vincent Spaulding want to rob?
　① the shop
　② the bank
　③ the Red-Headed League
　④ Sherlock Holmes

19. How were the busts made?
　① They were carved from a solid block of plaster.
　② They were made from several blocks of plaster, glued together.
　③ They were made from soft plaster, poured into molds and left to harden.
　④ They were shaped by hand from clay and coated with plaster.

20. Which of these was NOT in the dead man's pocket?
　① an apple
　② a photograph
　③ a map
　④ a knife

21. Choose *two* statements that are correct about the murder at Mr. Harker's
house.

   ① The stolen bust was found in the next street.

   ② The photograph was a picture of the dead man.

   ③ The stolen bust was broken into two halves.

   ④ The dead man had been stabbed with a knife.

22. Where did Holmes and his companions hide at the house of Mr. Brown in
Chiswick?

   ① up a tree

   ② round a corner

   ③ behind a rock

   ④ by a fence

23. Why did Sherlock Holmes write a letter to Mr. Sandeford?

   ① He accused Mr. Sandeford of a crime.

   ② He wanted to buy the bust of Napoleon from Mr. Sandeford.

   ③ He asked Mr. Sandeford to return a lost bag.

   ④ He invited Mr. Sandeford to examine the black pearl.

24. Which "do" was used differently from the others?

   ① I <u>do</u> hope you can help me.

   ② I <u>do</u> hope you meet me.

   ③ I <u>do</u> it every day.

   ④ I <u>do</u> know him.

25. What is the correct word for the blank?

> There were other chairs _____________ closer to you.

   ① very   ② many

   ③ much   ④ too

26. What is the correct sentence?
    ① It seemed that a short man.
    ② It seemed that he was a short man.
    ③ It seemed a short man.
    ④ He seemed that a short man.

※ Choose the wrong part of the sentence. (27~30)

27.
The <u>top</u> <u>floor</u> <u>is belonged</u> <u>to</u> Miles Mclaren.
    ① ②   ③   ④

28.
He <u>smashed</u> each one to pieces, <u>has hoped</u> <u>to find</u> the one in which
    ①   ②   ③

the pearl <u>was</u> hidden.
    ④

29.
<u>Only</u> a man as <u>taller</u> as Gilchrist would <u>be</u> able <u>to do</u> it.
 ①   ②   ③   ④

30.
It <u>was</u> empty <u>but for</u> <u>there was</u> two <u>wooden</u> chairs and a table.
   ①   ②   ③   ④

 Memo

Memo

Sarah J. Dodd
Sarah J. Dodd is an experienced primary school teacher who resides in the UK, but has also lived and taught in Australia. She has a PhD in Science and a certificate in Creative Writing. She has published several books for children: "An Angel Anyway" (Anyway Press, 2008), the "Little Angels" series (Lion Children's Books, 2009/10), "The Lion Picture Bible" (Lion Children's Books, 2015) and "Legs: the tale of a meerkat lost and found" (Lion Children's Books, 2015). Her poetry for children has also been highly commended and published in the anthology "Let in the Stars" (Manchester Metropolitan University, 2014).
She is currently working on further picture books for the very young, and a novel for older children.

Stories of Sherlock Holmes

Written by Sir Arthur Conan Doyle
Retold by Sarah J. Dodd
Illustrated by Gyeongmi Yang

First Published in May 2017

Editorial Manager: Juyon Choi
Editors: Juyon Choi, Kyunghee Jang, Jiyeong Park
Designers: Eunhee Lee, Elim
Cover Designer: Eunhee Lee

Published and distributed by

Darakwon Bldg., 64-1 Jandari-ro, Mapo-gu, Seoul, Korea 04031
Tel: 82-2-736-2031(ext. 250)   Fax: 82-2-732-2037
Homepage: www.ihappyhouse.co.kr
Publisher: Kyudo Chung

ISBN: 978-89-6653-526-2 18740 / 978-89-6653-156-1 18740(set)

[Components]
- 1 Audio CD (Recording Studio: Aram)
- Answer Keys & Korean Translation: Free download at www.ihappyhouse.co.kr